This book is gifted

To: _____

From: _____

Date:_____

To: Myah
From: Sam & Rita
Keep on shining!

Publisher: Burke's Publishing
Authors: Sam & Rita Burke
Illustrator: Md. Ashik

Published January 2022
ISBN: 978-0-9809963-2-6
https://ilikebeingmebooks.com
https://burkesbookstore.ca

Printed in Canada

I LIKE
BEING ME

I like being me, I like being me,
I like to hug myself and
feel the strength that comes
from deep inside of me.

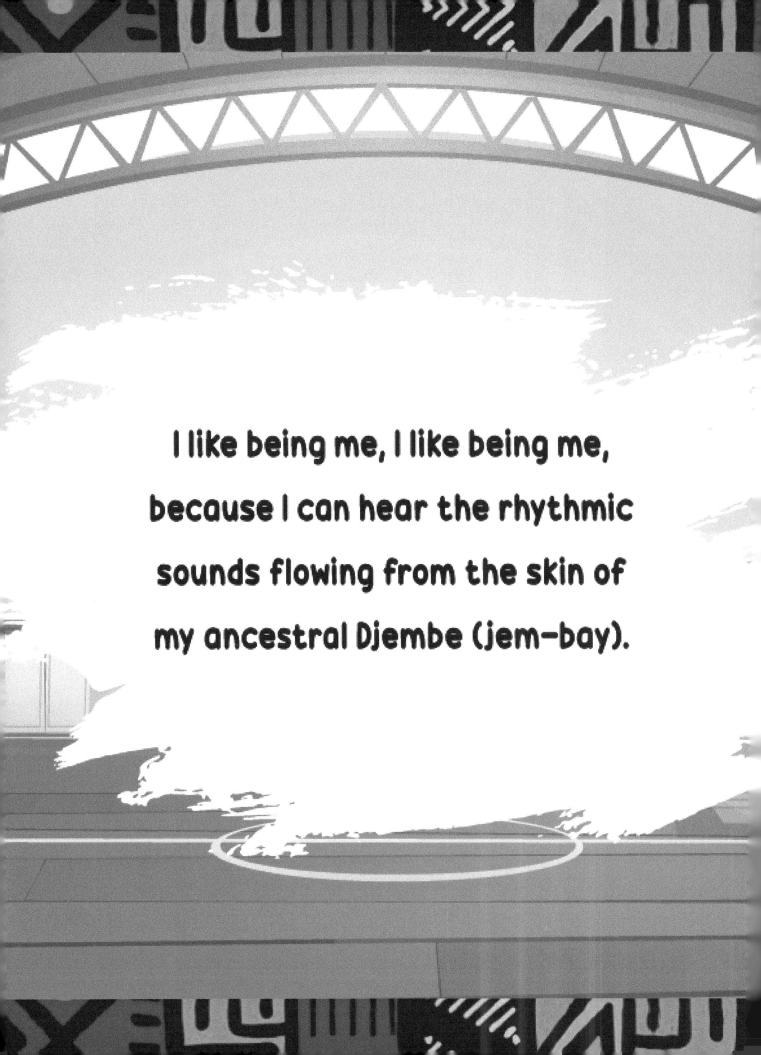

I like being me, I like being me, because I can hear the rhythmic sounds flowing from the skin of my ancestral Djembe (jem-bay).

YOU ARE CAPABLE

I like being me, I like being me, because I can see your sun-kissed smile as we eat sweet potato pie under the coconut tree.

I like being me, I like being me,
because I get to
taste delicious meals when
I visit my Aunt Tanti.

I like being me, I like being me,
because I can smell
the early morning freshness
of the deep blue sea.

I like being me, I like being me,

for even though I was born in

this land, I can proudly celebrate

the roots of my ancestry.

FAMILY TREE

I like being me, I like being me,
I now have the confidence to
start searching for the missing
branches of my family tree.

I like being me, I like being me,
do you like being you?
Even though you scored four
goals and I scored two?

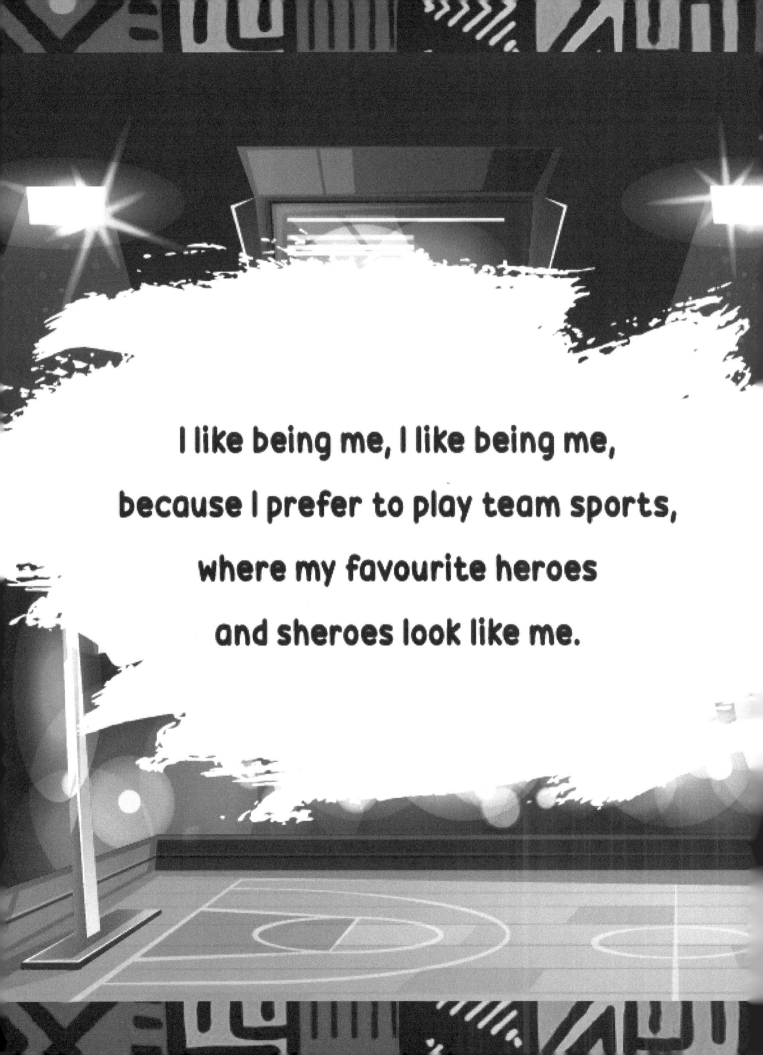

I like being me, I like being me,
because I prefer to play team sports,
where my favourite heroes
and sheroes look like me.

I like being me, I like being me, and I get excited when I read picture books and watch you enjoy your chapter books, but we can still be friends, even if we have different points of view.

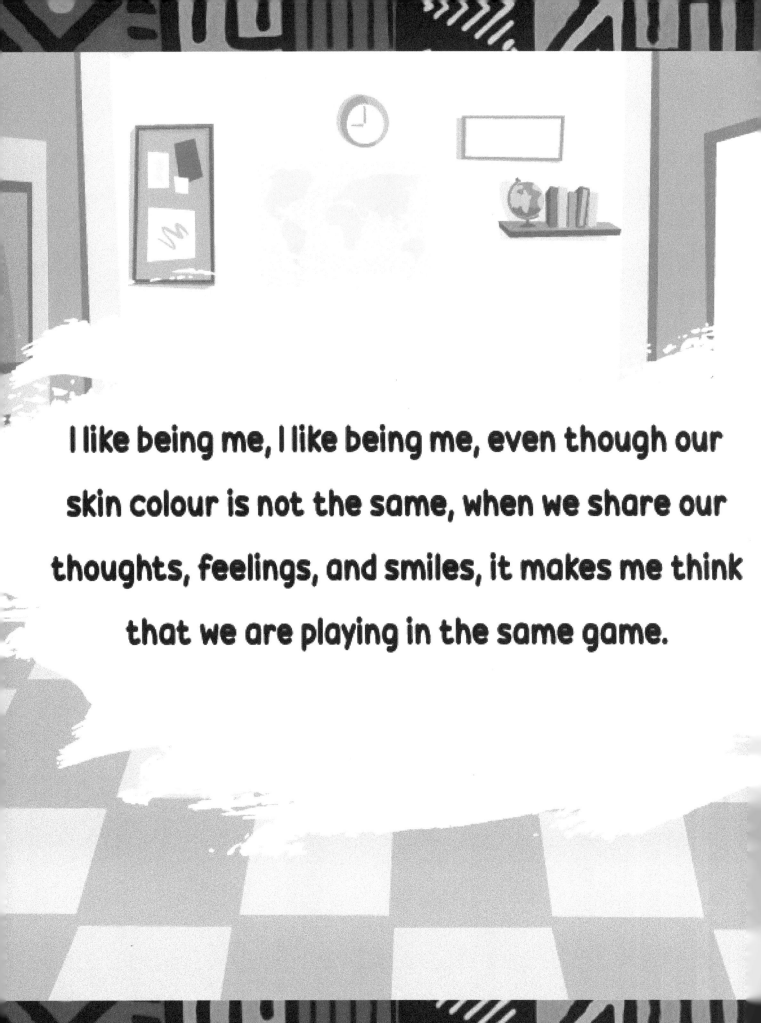

I like being me, I like being me, even though our skin colour is not the same, when we share our thoughts, feelings, and smiles, it makes me think that we are playing in the same game.

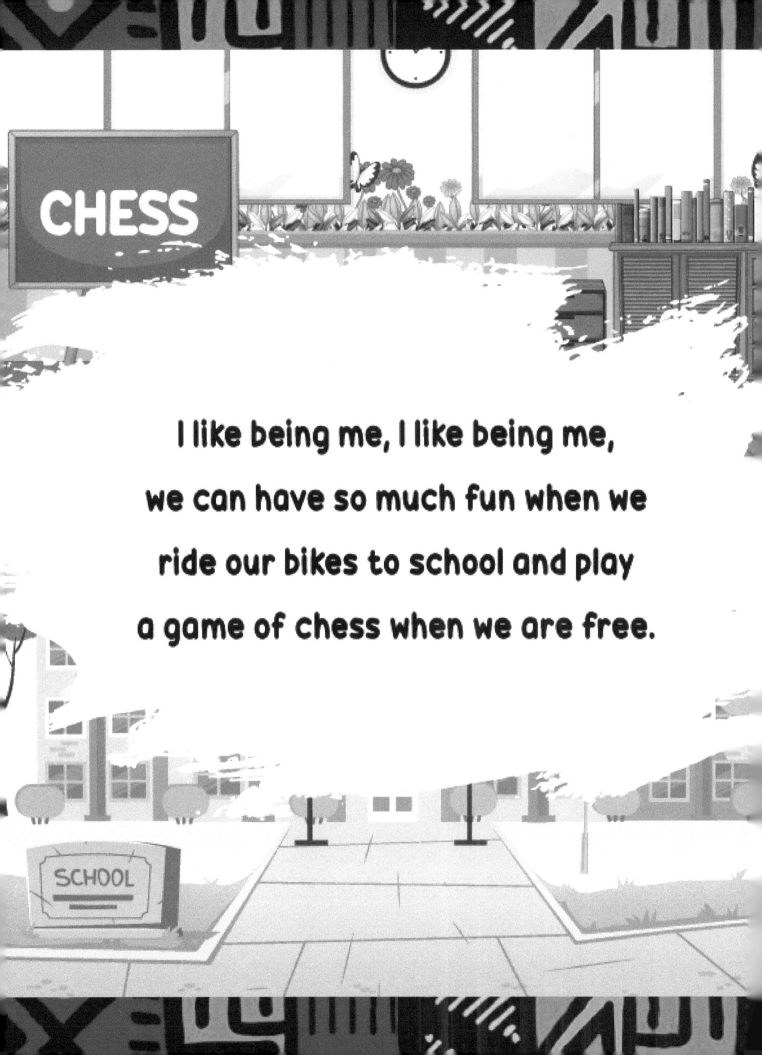

CHESS

I like being me, I like being me,
we can have so much fun when we
ride our bikes to school and play
a game of chess when we are free.

I like being me, I like being me, I like to read and I like to write, because my grandma and grandpa tell me that when I read and when I write I become confident and I become bright.

A   B   C   D

I LIKE BEING....

CONFIDENT	RESPECTFUL	KIND
CREATIVE	SPECIAL	GLAD
COURAGEOUS	HELPFUL	SMART

I can be happy, I can be sad, I can be creative,
courageous, confident, and glad.
But most of all, I like being me, I like being me,
I really, really, like being me.

THE END

Have fun filling in the names on your own family tree

FAMILY TREE

Have fun circling the words from the list below

M	T	Y	C	S	C	H	O	O	L	C	H	R	X	Z	N	M	T	O	A
D	H	T	G	N	E	R	T	S	B	N	C	H	E	S	S	B	F	T	L
B	R	S	C	Q	H	O	P	D	N	R	A	R	E	F	M	E	A	L	T
O	D	G	C	I	L	I	K	E	B	E	I	N	G	M	E	C	M	V	R
G	H	R	O	M	W	D	Q	L	P	C	C	S	R	Y	M	U	I	O	C
P	S	V	N	A	R	N	A	I	E	C	I	P	A	T	R	V	L	Y	G
C	O	N	F	I	D	E	N	C	E	O	R	X	N	D	E	T	Y	T	N
D	V	X	I	Q	Y	Z	R	I	U	S	A	T	D	C	T	N	S	Q	C
H	S	R	D	E	C	O	C	O	N	U	T	O	M	Z	P	Q	B	T	J
C	I	V	E	N	E	R	W	U	M	T	G	R	A	N	D	P	A	A	P
P	T	R	N	D	V	L	J	S	L	R	O	W	E	I	V	O	S	M	O
E	T	W	T	I	D	S	B	R	V	I	A	U	O	X	Y	P	K	C	T
N	U	N	D	E	N	D	R	A	C	W	L	X	U	G	A	M	E	O	A
O	U	M	S	K	I	N	D	X	P	B	S	M	B	Y	N	P	T	W	T
A	Q	H	E	R	O	E	S	H	U	A	I	L	R	M	E	Y	B	S	O
G	N	S	F	C	B	I	D	P	A	U	C	E	L	E	B	R	A	T	E
U	R	I	L	M	O	R	N	I	N	G	T	S	G	W	N	U	L	R	P
V	W	Q	E	E	Y	F	V	A	E	N	N	X	H	D	J	W	L	A	C
A	S	J	E	B	W	Z	Q	L	C	R	E	A	T	I	V	E	T	M	S
R	D	Q	X	B	J	L	F	E	E	L	I	N	G	S	F	O	N	S	D

- AUNT
- BASKETBALL
- BLUE
- BRIGHT
- CAPABLE
- CELEBRATE
- CHESS
- COCONUT
- CONFIDENCE
- CONFIDENT
- CREATIVE
- DELICIOUS
- DJEMBE
- DRUM
- END
- FAMILY
- FEELINGS
- FRIENDS
- GAME
- GOALS
- GRANDMA
- GRANDPA
- HEROES
- (I LIKE BEING ME)
- KIND
- MEAL
- MORNING
- POTATO
- SCHOOL
- SMART
- SOCCER
- STRENGTH
- TREE
- VIEW

Design your own book cover for the book I Like being Me

Put a circle around the number that shows how much you like being you. (10 is the highest)

1   2   3   4   5   6   7   8   9   10

I LIKE BEING ME
WORKBOOK

By Sam and Rita Burke
Illustrated by: Md. Ashik

Continue to enjoy I Like Being Me with the exciting activities in the Workbook.

Copies available at: https://Ilikebeingmebooks.com
or Contact - 1-647-638-7708

CPSIA information can be obtained
at www.ICGtesting.com
Printed in the USA
BVHW011143030223
657762BV00001B/2